ZEN

禅

ZEN

禅

A SHORT INTRODUCTION
WITH ILLUSTRATIONS
BY THE AUTHOR

ALAN WATTS

PREFACE BY
SHINGE ROKO SHERRY CHAYAT

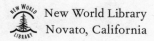
New World Library
Novato, California

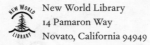 New World Library
14 Pamaron Way
Novato, California 94949

Text design by Tona Pearce Myers

Library of Congress Cataloging-in-Publication data is available.

Originally published in the United States in 1948 by James Ladd Delkin, Stanford, California
First New World Library printing, July 2019

ISBN 978-1-60868-588-2
Ebook ISBN 978-1-60868-589-9
Printed in Canada on 100% postconsumer-waste recycled paper

 New World Library is proud to be a Gold Certified Environmentally Responsible Publisher. Publisher certification awarded by Green Press Initiative.

10   9   8   7   6   5   4   3   2   1

CONTENTS

PREFACE

WITH ITS RADICALLY SIMPLE and direct title, *Zen* was among the earliest books by Alan Watts to intrigue spiritual seekers. This edition of *Zen*, appearing some seventy years after the original small printing, is sure to do the same for a new generation of readers. It offers a clear, concise, and informative introduction to a path that inspired Alan Watts from an early age and continued to intrigue him throughout his life.

Zen was published in England in 1947 under the title *Zen Buddhism: A New Outline and Introduction*. The American edition, published by James Ladd Delkin, came out in 1948, the same year as the second edition of Watts's *The Spirit of Zen*. "Since writing *The Spirit of Zen*...many valuable sources of information on the general nature of Zen have been available to me," Watts writes in his foreword to *Zen*, adding that the new book, "though brief, will in several important respects provide a corrective to the former volume."[*]

Among those "valuable sources" was D. T. Suzuki, as well as the Zen master Sokei-an Shigetsu Sasaki and his disciple Ruth Everett, who became Sasaki's wife in 1944, the year before his death. Ruth Everett was the mother of Eleanor Everett, who married Watts in 1938, two years after the first edition of *The Spirit of Zen*.

Precocious and intellectually adventuresome, Watts had been delving into Buddhist teachings even while in boarding school at King's School in Canterbury, England. After reading Lafcadio Hearn's *Glimpses of Unfamiliar Japan*, he borrowed from a friend *The Creed of Buddha* by Edmond Holmes, which contained a pamphlet written by Christmas Humphreys about the work of the Buddhist Lodge in London. Becoming a member and subscribing to the lodge's journal, *The Middle Way*, he submitted his first writing on Zen for publication.

As Alan's daughter Joan Watts writes in *The Collected Letters of Alan Watts*, on the basis of that essay he "was invited to speak to the members, who were shocked to learn that Alan Watts was a mere lad of fifteen."[†]

---

[*] See p. 17.

[†] Watts, *The Collected Letters of Alan Watts*, p. xiii.

Humphreys became his mentor, and it was through him that Watts met D. T. Suzuki. At around the same time, he exchanged letters with Sokei-an Sasaki, who wrote to the brilliant young seeker, "It is very hard to judge the ultimate attainment of Zen without observing the daily life and establishing a close contact between teacher and disciple in order to make certain whether attainment is one of mere conception or that of really standing in its center.... I am quite sure you are on the way of Zen and I hope some day in the future we will meet each other."[*]

That meeting took place in 1938, when Watts and his new wife, Eleanor, arrived in the United States. However, Watts himself never established the kind of connection with a Zen master that Sokei-an Sasaki had recommended, despite his mother-in-law's long immersion in traditional training at Nanzen-ji and years later at Daitoku-ji (where Ruth was ordained and installed as abbot of Ryosen-an, a sub-temple there) and her association, along with Sokei-an, with the First Zen Institute in New York and Kyoto.

For the young Watts, *Zen* was not only a corrective to *The Spirit of Zen*; it was a deeply personal response to what he saw as the shortcomings of Western metaphysics

---

[*]   Watts, *The Collected Letters of Alan Watts*, p. 8.

and, in particular, of Christianity. While writing *Zen*, Watts was preparing for ordination in the Episcopal Church, working as chaplain and living at Canterbury House at Northwestern University in Evanston, Illinois, with Eleanor and their young daughters, Joan and Anne.

From several letters of that period, it's clear that Watts viewed his engagement with Christianity as a means toward changing the Church from within. The revelations of oneness he found in Zen paralleled what he considered the most important truth of Christianity: the mystery of God. He equated the mystical in Christianity with the naturalness of Zen; the ineffability of God with the nowness of Zen awakening. Indeed, in an earlier book, *The Legacy of Asia and Western Man* (1937), he had called for "a Christianity reinforced by all that Asia (i.e., Buddhism, Taoism, Hinduism, etc.) can give."*

Writing *Zen* while taking on all the rituals and trappings of ecclesiastical Christianity must have been appealingly surreptitious. By the time of his ordination, he had grown impatient with the strictures of the Church and with what he felt was an untenable narrow-mindedness among its leaders. Two years after the US publication of *Zen*, he submitted his resignation to Bishop Wallace

---

*   Quoted in Watts, *The Collected Letters of Alan Watts*, p. 254.

Conkling with, as Joan Watts notes, "a barrage of criticism of the Church."* She quotes a letter to his friends in which he wrote, "During the past years I have continued my studies of the spiritual teachings of the Orient, alongside with Catholic theology, and, though I have sometimes doubted it, I am now fully persuaded that the Church's claim to be the best of all ways to God is not only a mistake, but also a symptom of anxiety."†

Zen presents an eminently accessible overview of Buddhist teachings, calling for the cessation of grasping and rejecting the inherent dualism of any intellectual formula. Rather than trying to possess God, he wrote, it was necessary to allow God — and life — to possess you. For Watts, to be fully alive was the essence of Zen; it could not be defined. How could one convey that essence? Only through immediate insight into the nature of Reality. It could only be transmitted, as Buddha did while holding up a flower, silently. Words would always and immediately lead to concepts, creating an intellectual divide between the nowness of spiritual experience and any attempt to define it.

Nonetheless, Watts was in love with words. Ever the

---

*   Watts, *The Collected Letters of Alan Watts*, p. 261.
†   Ibid.

scholar of comparative religions, he offers in *Zen* a brief overview of the Hindu Upanishads, early Indian Mahayana Buddhism, Chinese Taoism and Confucianism, and the development of Zen monastic practice in Tang dynasty China and in Japan, noting that Mahayana Buddhism was "somewhat infected with the characteristically Indian desire to escape from the world of form, but in China it lost this desire almost entirely."* Zen Buddhism, for Watts, was "the synthesis of the contemplative insight of Indian religion, the dynamic liveliness of Taoism, and the down-to-earthness of Confucianism."†

In the process of writing *Zen*, Watts was keenly aware of how quickly one can get entangled in dualism, warning his readers not to form "the *concept* of a pure and unchanging consciousness separate and apart from the changing forms of thoughts and things." He was encouraging the "perpetual self-abandonment" to the pure Mind, "an identification of itself with its changing forms, which in Christian language would be called the divine love." It's not "that we have to *make* the pure Mind perform this act of self-abandonment," he noted; "it does it by itself all the time, in us and through us."‡

---

* See p. 33.

† See p. 37.

‡ See pp. 48–49.

Zen's final section addresses the instantaneous action through self-abandonment found in the traditional Zen arts, whether in calligraphic brushstrokes or haiku, flower arranging or stone gardens, tea ceremony or archery — and the deep training and discipline necessary for that instantaneous action to be authentic.

It's remarkable how in such a slender volume — what he called his little booklet — Watts could convey Zen's challenges and its possibilities for life-changing breakthroughs. More than an outline or overview, *Zen* itself is like a haiku, a condensation of profundity that beckons to new understandings.

— Shinge Roko Sherry Chayat
Abbot of the Zen Studies Society, New York, 2019

FOREWORD

THE SUBSTANCE OF THIS ESSAY was first published in England in 1947 under the title *Zen Buddhism: A New Outline and Introduction*. The present American edition has been enlarged and revised with a view to providing an up-to-date and comprehensive outline of Zen Buddhism for the increasing number of students of a subject upon which all major works have long been out of print. Since writing *The Spirit of Zen* (London, 1936; reprinted 1948) many valuable sources of information on the general nature of Zen have been available to me, and the present work, though brief, will in several important respects provide a corrective to the former volume.

I am indebted, as ever, to Dr. D. T. Suzuki for his translations of original material, the greater part of those quoted being his unless otherwise indicated. I am also indebted for much general information upon the subject to the late Sokei-an Sasaki, Abbot of Jofuku-in, who lived and taught for many years in New York, though I do not wish to make him responsible for any of the opinions given lest they should be in error. Some of this information I owe also to Mrs. Sasaki, who let me read many of the manuscripts of his lectures and translations, and discussed them with me, though, for the same reason, I must not make her responsible either. It is a pleasure to me, however, to have this opportunity of expressing thanks to them all.

At the end of the book will be found a bibliography and an explanation of the drawings, symbols, and Chinese characters used as chapter headings.

Alan W. Watts,
Canterbury House, Evanston, Illinois, 1948

INTRODUCTION

THERE IS NOTHING THAT MEN DESIRE MORE than life — the fullness of life, Reality itself. In one form or another they try to possess it by every possible means, as happiness, as power, as joy, as wealth, as spiritual insight, and even as simple existence to which they cling with all their might for fear that it will be taken away. But one thing is certain: the harder you try to possess life, the faster it slips away from you, and the less you understand of its mystery. For life itself, whatever it may be, cannot be grasped in any form, whether of matter, of emotion, or of thought. The moment you try to hold it in a fixed form, you miss it. Water drawn from the stream is no longer living water, for it ceases to flow. This is what the Buddha meant in saying that the cause of all human misery was *trishna* or selfish craving, because *trishna* is the attempt to grasp life in some form, more especially in the form of one's own personal existence. Man can only become alive in the fullest sense when he no longer tries to grasp life, when he releases his own life from the stranglehold of possessiveness so that it can go free and be itself.

In practice, almost all religions are attempts to grasp the mystery of life in either an intellectual formula or an emotional experience. Wherever it may be found, higher religion involves the discovery that this cannot be done, and that therefore man must relax his fearful grip upon life or God and permit it to possess him as, in fact, it does all the time whether he knows it or not. Zen Buddhism is a unique example of this kind of higher religion, and because the word "Zen" indicates this very spiritual state of full liveliness and non-grasping, it is really impossible to define Zen. Nevertheless, Zen has a philosophical and religious history by means of which we can arrive at some suggestion of its meaning.

As a specific form of Buddhism, Zen is first found in China, being the peculiarly Chinese version of the kind of Buddhism which, according to tradition, was brought from India by the sage Bodhidharma in or about the year 527 CE. Bodhidharma's Buddhism was a variety of the Mahayana school, the Buddhism of northern India, which is to be distinguished from the Hinayana or Southern school of Buddhism now prevalent in Ceylon, Burma, and Siam. The latter is founded on the Buddha's teaching as preserved in the scriptures of the Pali language, whereas the former recognizes, in addition to these, certain Sanskrit scriptures of supposedly later date which are of a deeply metaphysical character.

Bodhidharma's variety of the Mahayana was known as Dhyana Buddhism, pronounced "Ch'an" in Chinese and "Zen" in Japanese, and though the nearest English equivalent of "Dhyana" is "contemplation" this term has acquired a static and even dreamy connotation quite foreign to Dhyana. Dhyana, Ch'an, or Zen means immediate insight into the nature of Reality or life. In China, Dhyana Buddhism was strongly influenced by Taoism and Confucianism, and, under the guidance of the practical mentality of the Chinese, emerged as the Zen we know today in the seventh century CE. The development of this distinctively Chinese form of Dhyana was largely the work of Hui-neng (or Wei-lang), whose *Tan-ching* or *Platform Sutra* is one of its most authoritative texts. From 713, when Hui-neng died, until the close of the thirteenth century, Zen flourished widely in China and exercised a profound effect on all branches of art and culture. Ei-sai brought it to Japan in 1191, where it may be found to this day in its most vital form and where, too, it has had an extremely far-reaching effect upon the national culture.*

---

* A somewhat different account of the history of Zen in China is given by Hu Shih in "The Development of Zen Buddhism in China," *Chinese Political and Social Review*, vol. 15, no. 4. Peiping, January 1932. He traces its origin back to Tao-seng (*d.* 434), a disciple of a school of Taoist interpreters of Yoga represented by Hui-yuan (*d.* 416) and Tao-an (*d.* 385). According to Hu Shih,

In brief, Zen accounts for itself in the following way. Gautama Siddhartha became the Buddha, the Enlightened One, as the result of a profound spiritual experience, an immediate knowledge of Reality, which he realized while meditating under the famous Bodhi Tree near Gaya in northern India. This knowledge, being ineffable, could never be put into words, and all the Buddha's verbal teaching was simply an indication or suggestion of its nature, a mere device (*upaya*) for awakening men to real insight. The knowledge itself was, however, directly and mysteriously passed on to Mahakasyapa, the Buddha's chief disciple, on an occasion when, instead of preaching a sermon, the Buddha silently held up a flower before his disciples. All stood nonplussed save Mahakasyapa, whose understanding smile brought this recognition from his master: "I have the most precious treasure, spiritual and transcendental, which this moment I hand over to you,

---

Bodhidharma arrived in Canton as early as 470, but, even so, found Tao-seng's Dhyana school already in existence. The account given above follows Suzuki in his *Essays in Zen Buddhism*, vol. 1, but at present there is insufficient material at hand to enable the occidental student to decide between Suzuki and Hu Shih. Suzuki's account follows the official version of the Zen school.

O venerable Mahakasyapa!" Tradition asserts that this knowledge was handed down from Mahakasyapa through a line of patriarchs to Bodhidharma, who brought it to China, where it continued to be passed from teacher to teacher. Because this knowledge can never be written down Zen does not rely on scriptures, even though it may use them as devices. Words cannot convey it, just as they cannot describe colors to a blind man. Thus Zen is summed up as:

A special transmission [of insight] outside the scriptures;
No dependence upon words and letters;
Direct pointing to the soul of man;
Seeing into one's own nature.

To understand Zen adequately, however, we must realize that it is the fruit and synthesis of the most important trends in both Indian and Chinese religion.

THE BACKGROUND
IN INDIAN RELIGION

INDIAN RELIGION HAS EVER BEEN CHARACTERIZED
by the quest for "that One thing, knowing which we
shall know all." In the Upanishads this "One thing" is
termed Brahman, the absolute Reality of the universe
beyond all opposites. All ordinary things and experiences have opposites; life is opposed to death, pleasure
to pain, joy to sorrow, light to darkness. These opposites are necessary to one another, so that life is always

limited by death, and joy by sorrow. But Reality itself has no opposite; it is *advaita*, non-dual, and the soul of man is only delivered from death and sorrow by realizing its identity with Reality. For the Upanishads taught that Brahman is the true nature of ourselves and of all things. Not to realize this is ignorance (*avidya*) and unhappiness, but to know it is true knowledge (*vidya*) and a transcendental happiness which is eternal because, strange to say, it too has no opposite. Thus the religion of the Upanishads was more or less monistic, believing that all forms and objects were in fact manifestations of the One Absolute.

Primitive Indian Buddhism also sought this Reality, but its way of approach was purely psychological. The Buddha felt that philosophical speculation about Reality was a waste of time and even a positive hindrance. Reality or Nirvana lay beyond all definition, and nothing was of importance but an immediate and intimate experience of it, and this could only be had by getting rid of *trishna*. Reality is here and now, but it is concealed by attempts to grasp it in this form or that.

Later Indian Buddhism, which is to say Mahayana, linked both the psychological approach of primitive Buddhism and the metaphysical tradition of the Upanishads. But whereas the Upanishads described the non-dual Reality as the One, Mahayana felt this term misleading. One is opposed to Many and None, for which reason Reality must transcend even oneness. Mahayana went beyond monism, and certainly beyond any trace of that Spinozist pantheism so often, and, it may be said, erroneously, attributed to the Upanishads. To say that all things are one is to reduce everything to something which is still short of non-duality, since, as we have seen, one-ness has an opposite and so cannot be the Absolute. Furthermore, the very statement, "All things are Reality," contains an *implied* opposition between "all things" and "Reality." In making such a statement we are uniting two things which are in no need of union. They are already united, and to try to *create* the union in thought or in feeling is to imply to oneself that it does not already exist. Nirvana (the state of Reality) *is* Samsara (the state of ordinary life) and the very act of trying to realize that they are one implies that they are not. In any case, Reality is not one; it is non-dual, having no opposite at all.

Therefore Mahayana spoke of Reality as Tathata, or Thusness, and as Sunyata, or the Void, considered not as mere emptiness but as "solid emptiness." Sunyata resembles a crystal ball, which is visible to our eyes only because of what it reflects. Hold it up before a crowded street, and there within it is a crowded street. Hold it up before the empty sky, and there seems to be nothing in it, but only because it is reflecting the emptiness of the sky. Its true nature remains unknown. As the crystal ball reflects images, the manifold universe appears spontaneously within Sunyata. There is nothing in it, but everything comes out of it. Sunyata is the all-inclusive; having no opposite, there is nothing which it excludes or opposes. This was a philosophical theory expressing a spiritual and psychological state — the state of non-grasping or freedom from *trishna*. To thought and sense and feeling Reality is a void, for they cannot lay hold on it or keep it in any fixed form. But it is a living void, because all forms come out of it, and whoever realizes it is filled with life and power and the Bodhisattva's love (*karuna*)* for all beings.

From a somewhat more psychological standpoint, Sunyata is also regarded as the ground of human consciousness — the "essence of Mind," the supra-individual Self, in which all our varying states of consciousness, our thoughts, emotions, and sensations have their being, like images produced spontaneously in a mirror. This production of images is held to be playful rather than purposive, as if in the act of "creation" Reality were simply enjoying itself — an idea resembling the Hindu view of the universe as the *lila*, the playful dance, of God. Thus Mahayana considers Reality under three aspects which, somewhat in the manner of the Persons of the Christian Trinity, are in essence one: Dharmakaya, which is the pure and undifferentiated Sunyata; Sambhogakaya, which is the creative principle of enjoyment, the *lila*; and Nirmanakaya, which is the resultant manifested universe.

---

*   *Karuna* is the moral equivalent of all-inclusiveness.

THE BACKGROUND
IN CHINESE RELIGION

WHILE ZEN DERIVED its highly practical approach to religion from Confucianism, it was actually more deeply influenced by Taoism as taught by Lao-tzu (sixth century BCE) and Chuang-tzu (third century BCE). In Taoism Reality is termed Tao, another untranslatable word, which has, however, a rather more dynamic connotation than Brahman, Tathata, or Sunyata. Tao is life considered as a *flowing* power, like the wind, or a stream, or the present moment. It is sometimes rendered as "the Way of things," or as the Logos. A person who has realized union with Tao is said to be in a state of Te, or "grace," while the method of realization is called Wu-wei (no-assertion), which is highly similar to the Buddhist idea of giving up *trishna*. As in Buddhism, all evils are attributed to man's self-assertiveness, his itch to possess life in fixed forms. But if he can realize that he is one with Tao, the fullness of life, he will cease to want to possess things and will therefore be free from evil. If man ceases from self-assertion and lets go of life, the Tao will have a chance to operate freely within him. His life will be lived not by his own ego, but by Tao.

While Indian religion made its object the realization of man's identity with Brahman or Tathata, of the inherent unity of appearance and Reality, Samsara and Nirvana, Chinese religion made its object harmony with the Tao. To Indian religion, the result of this realization was that man was delivered from the realm of opposites, that is, from life and death as we know them. His consciousness passed from the state of manifestation into the state of absolute Reality. Chinese religion was not in quite so much of a hurry to separate consciousness from everyday life. Man was in harmony with Tao here and now, fully in possession of his ordinary everyday consciousness of people and things. In principle, Mahayana Buddhism was at one with Taoism in this respect, for in insisting that there was no real difference between Nirvana and Samsara it could not allow the idea of *passing* from one to the other. Mahayana was, however, somewhat infected with the characteristically Indian desire to escape from the world of form, but in China it lost this desire almost entirely. It became a world-transforming instead of a world-escaping religion.

Despite superficial differences, it will be seen that these two trends of Indian and Chinese religion have a common essence. Hindu-Buddhist religion discovered the essential Reality of life through detachment from its particular forms, assisted by the practice of meditation. Taoism discovered the essential harmony of everyday life with Tao by letting go of that life so that it could be free to be itself.

Both procedures are grounded in a common faith or trust, namely, that this everyday life *is* Reality, that all things *are* in harmony with Tao, and that therefore this will be clear to you if you simply let go of the possessive itch. To try to *attain* union with Reality by action or by inaction (which is simply an indirect form of action) is to imply that you do not already have that union. There is nothing to be attained. The union simply *is*; Samsara *is* Nirvana. The effort to attain something is just another form of that acquisitive desire which springs from lack of trust in the one supreme fact. In the words of Hsi-yun:

> By their very seeking for it they produce the contrary effect of losing it, for that is using the Buddha to seek for the Buddha and using mind to grasp mind. Even though they do their utmost for a full kalpa [aeon], they will not be able to attain to it.... If it is held that there is something to be attained apart from

mind and, thereupon, mind is used to seek it, [that implies] failure to understand that mind and the object of its search are one.*

---

* *The Huang Po Doctrine of Universal Mind*. Trans. by Chu Ch'an. London, 1947, pp. 16 and 24. The term "mind" as used here signifies that ground of consciousness or mind-essence which, as explained above, is identical with Sunyata.

THE MOMENTOUS HARMONY

HISTORICALLY, ZEN IS THE EMBODIMENT of the common truth contained in the Hindu-Buddhist tradition and the Taoist tradition, the synthesis of the contemplative insight of Indian religion, the dynamic liveliness of Taoism, and the down-to-earthness of Confucianism. Zen is grounded precisely in this faith or trust that ordinary life is Tao, and is to be accepted or loved as such. The Zen master Chao-chu was asked,

"What is the Tao?" He replied, "Everyday life is the Tao." "How," pursued the inquirer, "does one get into harmony with it?" "If you *try* to get into harmony with it, you will get away from it." The attempt suggests the absence of the Reality, and proceeds from lack of faith in the truth that harmony already is. Lack of faith in this harmony creates the sense of inadequacy and insecurity which underlies all our aggressive and evil actions.

But Zen is more than a synthesis of these various trends in Indian and Chinese religion. The unique contribution of Zen to higher religion is its method of presenting the truth, a method involving "No dependence on words and letters, and direct pointing to the soul of man" — that is, to the Tao, Buddha-nature, or Reality itself.

It is all too easy for ideas and concepts to conceal rather than reveal Reality. Thus the Zen masters say that ideas are fingers pointing at the moon of Reality, but that most people mistake the finger for the moon. Furthermore, we have already seen that it is quite impossible for ideas to describe or convey the deepest truth of life, since ideas are forms and Reality is too living to be held in any form. Zen, therefore, does not consist in acquiring new ideas about Reality and our relation to it; it consists in getting rid of ideas and feelings *about* life in order that we may get to life itself. The statement that ordinary life is Tao, or that we are one with Reality just as we are, here and now, is still an idea, and while it remains an idea it is still an attempt to capture the living truth in a fixed formula. Really to understand Zen we have to get away from this abstract and dead realm of concepts and come face-to-face with Reality as it stands quite clearly before us here and now.

There is only one place where we are truly alive, where we come into immediate contact with Reality, and that is *now* — this present moment. The past was only real when it was the present moment, and the future will only be real when it becomes it. The past continues to be real to the extent that it lives on effectually in the present. But real life is always now. In fact, we have no knowledge of any other reality than the present moment, and, strictly speaking, nothing has any existence save in this moment. Yet what we call the present moment is strangely elusive. As soon as we try to catch hold of it, it seems to run away. We cannot delay or hold it in any of the forms which it assumes or contains. We have moments of pleasure and moments of pain, but when we try to grab hold of the moment of pleasure, the moment, the movement, the life leaves the pleasure and it turns to dust in our hands. So, too, when we try to examine the moment, we cannot discover it, for it is too small to see. The more we look for it, the tinier it becomes, until we realize that it is infinitesimal and thus infinite.

Yet however much we may try to delay or grasp the moment, the fact remains that while, from one point of view, it eludes us, from another, we cannot get away from it. We may try to lag behind in the past or to hurry on into the future, but inevitably we do our lagging or hurrying in the present moment. As soon as we realize that the moment is in reality inescapable, we shall no longer try to grasp it; for whether we know it or not, it grasps us. For the now, this present moment, is Reality. All things proceed from it and exist in it, and yet when we look at it directly it seems nothing. Now is Tao, and Tao is now, and even though we do our damnedest to possess it, we are still unable to get out of it. Our union with Reality is the truth whether we realize it or not, whether we strive to attain it or not.

But to say that the now is Tao, or is Reality, at once introduces a concept which, useful though it may be for a time, instantly distracts our attention from the real now. At once our religion becomes dead and removed from life, for although this now, this eternal moment, looks so void and so uninteresting to sense and thought, in fact it is the mysterious source of all liveliness and power. The genius of Zen lies in its way of pointing to the real now without distracting the attention with concepts. But the human mind, because of its inherently possessive nature, lets go of concepts with extreme reluctance, for which reason Zen has sometimes to attack and smash them quite violently. Thus its technique has often the appearance of spiritual shock tactics.

DIRECT POINTING

THE ZEN WAY OF TEACHING is to demonstrate Reality rather than to talk about it, or, if words are used at all, to avoid formally religious terminology and conceptual statements. When Zen speaks it expresses Reality, not with logical explanations and doctrines but with everyday conversation, or with statements that upset the normal conceptual mode of thinking so violently that they appear as utter nonsense. Because

Zen desires to get rid of concepts, to shatter the rigid frames in which we try to possess life, it employs a thoroughgoing iconoclasm. At the same time, Zen as a formal religious cult reads the scriptures, uses images and ceremonies, and sometimes breaks down far enough to include sermons and explanations. But it is just the preservation of this formal aspect of religion which makes the informal and iconoclastic such a puzzling and effective contrast, a truth which Western reformers and iconoclasts have never appreciated.

The greater part of Zen literature consists of *mondo*, of brief dialogues between masters and pupils, which illustrate its peculiar method of instruction, pointing to the real now without interposing ideas and notions about it. Here, for example, is the way in which Zen deals with the problem of non-duality, concerning which Indian Buddhism has composed so many volumes of intricate explanation.

A monk asked Dosan, "How do we escape the heat when summer comes and the cold when winter is here?"

The master said, "Why not go where there is no summer, no winter?"

"Where is such a place?"

"When the cold season comes, one is thoroughly chilled; when the hot summer is here, one swelters."

As to escaping from Samsara, the world of opposites and everyday consciousness, to Nirvana, the realm of absolute unity and peace, Zen has this to say:

Bokuju was once asked, "We have to dress and eat every day, and how can we escape from all that?"

The master replied, "We dress; we eat."

"I do not understand."

"If you do not understand, put on your dress and eat your food."

Or again:

"Pray show me the way to deliverance."

"Who has ever put you in bondage?"

"Nobody."

"If so, why should you ask for deliverance?"

Another master deals with this question rather more explicitly, but we must be careful that he does not fool us:

Hui-hai was asked, "How can one attain the Great Nirvana?"

"Have no karma that works for transmigration."*

"What is the karma for transmigration?"

"To seek after the Great Nirvana, to abandon the defiled and take to the undefiled, to assert that there is something attainable and something realizable, not to be free from the

---

* Karma (literally, action) is the law of causality, and thus the phrase "karma that works for transmigration" means the kind of action which has the effect of binding the agent to Samsara, where, according to general Buddhist belief, man is born again and again into the world until he realizes Nirvana.

teaching of opposites — this is the karma that works for transmigration."

"How can one be emancipated?"

"No bondage from the very first, and what is the use of seeking emancipation? Act as you will, go on as you feel — without second thought. This is the incomparable way."

Hui-hai's final remark must not, however, give the impression that Zen is just living lazily and fatuously in the present and taking life as it comes. If this be used as a formula for grasping the reality of Zen, the whole point is missed. A master was asked, "What is the Tao?" "Walk on!" he shouted. Thus whenever you think you have the right idea of Zen, drop it and walk on.

More and more we shall see that the essence of Zen is simply the giving up of any attempt to grasp life in ideational or emotional forms. It involves a thorough-going acceptance of life and experience just as it is at any given moment, which, whether we know it or not, is precisely what our basic, mirror-like consciousness is doing all the time. Passion, anger, elation, depression, ideas of good and evil, mine and yours — these are varying forms taken by our feelings and thoughts, whereas the essence of Mind, the essential consciousness, is ever formless, free, and pure. "The perfect man," said Chuang-tzu, "employs his mind as a mirror; it grasps nothing, it refuses nothing, it receives, but does not keep." At the same time, this must not lead us to form the *concept* of a pure and unchanging consciousness separate and apart from the changing forms of thoughts and things. The point is not at all to reject phenomena and cling to the Absolute, because the very nature of the Absolute, of the essential Mind, is non-clinging. As soon as we conceive a formless Self or mind-essence underlying and distinct from the changing contents of experience, we are denying the very nature of that Self. For its nature is not to separate itself from anything, not to stand apart from experience but to accept and identify itself with it. Its very life and power consist in a perpetual self-abandonment to its varied experiences, an identification of itself with its changing forms, which in Christian language would be called the divine love. Nor must it be thought that we have to *make* the pure Mind perform this act of self-abandonment; it does it by itself all the time, in us and through us, whether we wish it or not.

This, then, is why Hui-neng constantly insisted that the only difference between an ordinary man and a Buddha, an enlightened one, is that the latter knows he is a Buddha whereas the former does not. When asked, "What is enlightenment?" a master replied, "Your everyday mind." "When a thought moves," wrote Kaku-an, "another follows, and then another — an endless train of thoughts is thus awakened. Through enlightenment all this turns into truth." In reality the enlightened consciousness is not different from our ordinary everyday consciousness; to seek it as something over and above our mind as it is at this moment is immediately to set up a dualism. We thrust realization from us in the very act of regarding it as something to be attained. This seeming paradox is aptly expressed by Ma-tsu:

In the Tao there is nothing to discipline oneself in. If there is any discipline in it, the completion of such discipline means the destruction of the Tao. But if there is no discipline whatever in the Tao, one remains an ignoramus.

It is only through seeking enlightenment that we find there is no need to seek. He goes on:

One thought follows another without interruption; the preceding one does not wait for the succeeding; each one is self-contained and quiescent. This is called the "Meditation of the Ocean-stamp," in which are included all things, like the ocean where all the rivers however different in size empty themselves.*

Whether we know it or not, the "ocean" of pure consciousness perfectly accepts the stream of our thoughts and impressions all the time. At every instant we are

---

* Suzuki, *Manual of Zen Buddhism*, pp. 126–127.

in complete harmony with the Tao, but an apparent discord arises when, through a wrong use of memory and anticipation, we allow past and future experiences to conflict with the present. In the words of Emerson:

> These roses under my window make no reference to former roses or to better ones; they are for what they are; they exist with God today. There is no time to them. There is simply the rose; it is perfect in every moment of its existence.... But man postpones or remembers; he does not live in the present, but with reverted eye laments the past, or, heedless of the riches that surround him, stands on tiptoe to foresee the future. He cannot be happy and strong until he too lives with nature in the present, above time.*

But between the unconscious harmony of the rose and the conscious harmony of the perfect man lies the

---

* *Essays*, First Series. "Self-Reliance."

illusion of self-consciousness, separation, and discord, wherein we strive blindly for what in truth we have never lost. Yet this itself is no more an *actual* loss of the Tao than the disappearance of the rose in winter is a violation of its natural and proper life. The bloom is forgotten and the seed goes underground. "Unless a grain of corn falls into the earth and dies," said Jesus, "it remains alone; but if it dies, it bears much fruit." In spiritual development there must always be the middle stage wherein by apparent loss, by seeking and striving, we become conscious of the harmony that is our unconscious possession all along.

> Before a man studies Zen, to him mountains are mountains and waters are waters; after he gets an insight into the truth of Zen through the instruction of a good master, mountains to him are not mountains and waters are not waters; but after this when he really attains to the abode of rest, mountains are once more mountains and waters are waters.[*]

---

[*] Ch'ing-yuan, in Suzuki, *Essays in Zen*, vol. 1, p. 12.

The ignoramus, the primitive "simple" man, accepts life for what it is, just as it comes. The "seeker," however, looks for the God, the Reality, the absolute and eternal consciousness behind life, regarding the images of ordinary experience as a distracting illusion. But the perfect man, consciously one with the Tao, again accepts life for just what it is.

> T'an asked a student, "What were you before you became a monk?"
> "I used to be a cowherd."
> "How do you look after the cattle?"
> "I go out with them early in the morning and come home when it grows dark."
> "Splendid is your ignorance!"

Zen is spiritual freedom or spiritual poverty, that is, the liberation of our true nature (Buddha-nature or essence of Mind) from the burden of those fixed ideas and feelings about Reality which we accumulate through fear — the fear that life will run away from us. "Scholars," said Lao-tzu, "gain every day;

but Taoists lose every day." Or in the words of Jesus, "Blessed are the poor in spirit, for theirs is the kingdom of heaven.... Blessed are the pure [i.e., naked and free] in heart, for they shall see God." Such poverty and freedom are expressed in this poem from the *Mumon-kan*:*

> Hundreds of spring-flowers; the autumn moon;
> A fresh summer breeze; winter snow:
> Free your mind from idle thoughts,
> And for you any season is a good season.

But again, we must "walk on" even from spiritual poverty if this be used as a means to *grasp* the truth of Zen. Chao-chu was asked, "What would you say to one who comes to you with nothing?" "Throw it away!"

These *mondo* may seem puzzling to the uninitiated, but in fact there is nothing obscure or hidden

---

* The *Mumon-kan* (Chinese, *Wu-men Kwan*) or "No Gate Barrier" is a standard collection of *mondo* with brief comments and poems about each. In the verse quoted here "idle thoughts" are fixed concepts.

about them. The truth which they indicate is, however, of such radical simplicity and self-evidence that
our complex and burdened minds find it hard to see.

> It is so clear that it takes long to see.
> You must know that the fire which you are
>   seeking
> Is the fire in your own lantern,
> And that your rice has been cooked from the
>   very beginning.*

Or, as Pai-chang said when asked how to find Reality,
"It is very much like looking for an ox when you are
riding on one."

> Kozankoku, a Confucian, came to Kwaido to ask
> about the hidden teaching of Zen. Kwaido said,
> "There is a passage in the text you are so thor-
> oughly familiar with, which fitly describes the

---

* *Mumon-kan*, vii. I am indebted for this translation to the Ven. Sokei-an
Sasaki, late abbot of Jofuku-in.

teaching of Zen. Did not Confucius declare, 'Do you think I am holding something back from you, O my disciples? Indeed, I have held nothing back from you.' "

Kozankoku could not understand this, and vainly pressed the master for a further explanation. But later, when they were walking together in the mountains, they passed a bush of wild laurel.

"Do you smell it?" asked Kwaido.

"Yes."

"There, I have kept nothing back from you!"

It would be fatal, however, to interpret this in a sentimentally pantheistic sense, as if Kwaido were saying that the smell of the wild laurel is the Tao. No such conceptualism enters here. Pantheism, deism, theism, monism, dualism — all these are intellectual forms which must fail to grasp the living Reality. But when this has been thoroughly understood, intellectual forms may be used again without captivating the mind.

Strictly speaking, Zen does not have a method for awakening our minds to Reality, unless it may be called a "method of no-method." A method, a technique for discovering Reality implies an attempt to grasp it, and this, according to Zen, is as misleading and unnecessary as "putting legs on a snake" or "adding frost over snow." In the words of Lin-chi:

> The true man who has an insight into Reality... gives himself up to all manners of situations in which he finds himself in obedience to his past karma. He appears in whatever garments are ready for him to put on. As it is desired of him either to move or to sit quietly, he moves or sits. He has not a thought of running after Buddhahood. He is free from such pinings. Why is it so with him? Says an ancient sage, "When the Buddha is sought after, he is the cause of transmigration."*

---

* Trans. D. T. Suzuki, *Essays in Zen Buddhism*, vol. iii, pp. 32–33. A free rendering of the original Chinese. Buddhahood is the state of enlightenment or awakening, or the immediate knowledge of Reality. Buddha is often used as a synonym for Reality.

ZEN MEDITATION

WHILE, FROM ONE POINT OF VIEW, Zen has no method, from another it has a definite technique of meditation. It is against this background of definite technique that the "method of no-method" has its value as a surprising contrast. The success of Zen lies in its freedom both to use technique and to dispense with it; it is not bound to any one-sided procedure.

The Zen way of meditation, known as *za-zen*, is the result of a long process of development.

Zen has always been a semi-monastic religion, though Zen monks do not take life vows, because many of them remain in the monastery only for a period of training before going back into the world as secular priests or laymen. In some ways these institutions resemble our theological seminaries rather than monasteries in the strict sense. Originally Zen "monasteries" were small groups of monks gathered around an approved *roshi* or master, whose way of handling them was relatively informal and spontaneous. The early *mondo* are simply records of the daily life and teaching of these primitive communities. Before long, however, these *mondo* were collected and some of them were used as formal koans, or subjects for meditation. Monks devoted part of their time to meditation, and part to manual work in support of the community, a way of life somewhat like the rule of St. Benedict.

In meditation the monk sits cross-legged in the

"lotus posture" (*padmasana*), and by slow, rhythmic breathing brings his mind to a state of calm and freedom from ideas. He then takes up his *koan* and drops it into his mind like a stone into a still pool, whereafter he simply watches its effect. Some of the famous koans are these: "Before father and mother, what is your true nature?" or, as we might word it, "Beyond time and space, what is Reality?" "What is the sound of your hand?" "Stop the booming of the distant bell" — how can this be done? "When asked, 'What is Buddha?' Ummon answered, 'Dried dung!'" — what does this mean?* Sometimes the *koan* seem to contradict each other. When asked, "What is Buddha?" Ba-so answered, "This mind is Buddha," but on another occasion he said, "This mind is not Buddha."

At regular intervals the monk goes to the *roshi* for an interview (*sanzen*) when he is expected to demonstrate his view of the *koan* assigned to him. This is not to be done by wordy explanation, but by some kind

---

*   Ummon's answer is sometimes translated, "The dried-up dirt scraper."

of direct action or direct pointing to Reality in the true Zen style. The *roshi* responds in the same way, sometimes with a laconic comment, sometimes with silence, sometimes with a bang on the head from the big stick which lies before him — for all these measures are parts of his spiritual shock tactics. Usually the monk sees into the meaning of his *koan* suddenly, experiencing a flash of insight termed *satori*, and this may occur during meditation, during *sanzen*, or while he is going about his ordinary work. For we see into Reality suddenly just because there is no real method or succession of stages for approaching it.

There are some 1,700 koans, and approximately fifty are needed for a full Zen training. It would seem that the various types of koans are used for getting rid of different types of conceptualism and mental fixation, and thus for revealing different "aspects" of the full understanding of Zen. More advanced koans have to do with the way in which Reality manifests itself in life and action. But it is almost impossible to discuss this subject with profit, since experiment alone can make sense of it. In the course of centuries *koan* meditation has become an art of the deepest subtlety, though much may be learned from the general attitude of Zen quite apart from work with *za-zen*.

THE CULTURAL EFFECTS
OF ZEN

ZEN HAS ENTERED INTO MANY ASPECTS of the life of the Far East — painting, architecture, gardening, chivalry, tea ceremony, etiquette, poetry, and ethics. Zen affects every sphere of daily life from the state-craft of the ruler to the menial work of the laborer. As a Zen poet says:

How wondrous, how miraculous, this —
I draw water and I carry fuel!

Its moral effects are profound but not obvious, for the oriental idea of goodness is not so self-conscious and self-assertive as the occidental. As Lao-tzu said, the wise man hides his virtue and appears on the surface like a fool, for "true grace [Te] does not appear as grace, and thus is grace; false grace is so aware of itself as grace that it is not grace." Zen produces thousands of Bodhisattvas who do not advertise themselves.

The most obvious effects of Zen are in the realm of aesthetics, for Chinese art of the T'ang, Sung, and Yuan periods, the Japanese painting of Sesshu and the Sumiye school, the gardening art of Kobori Enshiu, the haiku poetry of Basho and others — all these have had direct inspiration from Zen, or from a Zen-flavored Taoism. Three major characteristics of Far Eastern art exemplify aspects of the Zen life:

1. Absence of symmetry. The phenomena of nature are rarely symmetrical in form; at most there is only an approximation to absolute symmetry, and Zen perceives in this fact the lively and dynamic quality of nature. For symmetry is a state of such perfect balance that movement is no longer possible; a form so

balanced is dead, and thus the symmetrical form is analogous to that mental and emotional fixation which in Zen is ever broken down. It is for this reason that Chinese and Japanese paintings are so seldom architectural and wooden. There is no feeling at all of stuffing and the glass case in their drawings of birds, and the very rocks and mountains seem to flow. As a Western poet has said:

The hills are shadows, and they flow
From form to form, and nothing stands.

2. The use of emptiness. As Zen perceives the forms of life within Sunyata, the all-inclusive mystery of the Void, Chinese painting makes the greatest use of the empty background, of large expanses of mist, to suggest depth. For the empty spaces of Chinese painting are no *mere* emptiness; they are creative and suggestive, exciting the imagination and giving a startling clarity and vividness to the objects drawn against and within them. Zen taste deplores the cluttering of a picture or of a room with many objects. It likes to take

an empty space, and, within it, concentrate attention on one point — like the *koan* thrown into the still pool of the mind, like the one point of the living moment within the emptiness of past and future.

3. The instantaneous quality. This might be called, too, the momentary quality, for Chinese and Japanese art love to portray moments of life, as if the painter had just glimpsed his subject for a second. A duck is painted just in the act of alighting, or a spray of bamboos caught in a sudden gust of wind. The very media of the art — brush, ink, and silk or absorbent paper — require a swift, evenly flowing technique. As in life itself, a stroke once made can never be retouched. Zen, as Suzuki points out,

> permits no ossification as it were of each moment. It takes hold of each moment as it is born from Sunyata, that is, Emptiness, according to Buddhist philosophy. Momentariness is therefore characteristic of this philosophy. Each moment is absolute, alive, and signif-icant. The frog leaps, the cricket sings...a

breeze passes through the pine branches... Buddhism is quick to catch each movement of nature and expresses its impressions in a seventeen syllable poem or in a few strokes of the brush.*

---

* *Buddhist Philosophy and Its Effects on the Life and Thought of the Japanese People*, Kokusai Bunka Shinkokai, Tokyo, 1936, p. 26.

CONCLUSION

THE OCCIDENTAL READER must not gather from the foregoing that Zen is an easy-going aestheticism, a philosophy of idling along with the stream of events. Zen has also been the religion of warriors who applied it on the battlefield in the very moment of danger:

> Under the sword raised high
> Is hell, making you tremble.

But walk on! —
And there is the Land of Bliss.

The momentariness of Zen lies above and beyond the two wrong extremes of idling and hurrying, in an amazing poise, not of rigidity, but of balance in motion, not of the statue but of the dancer. For this is the balance of living Reality itself, of the unmoved Mover, of the whirlwind with peace at the heart.

In essence, Zen involves no doctrine. It is an experience of Reality beyond doctrine, for which reason Zen may be of use to people of any religion. It is to be doubted, however, whether one can ground one's life in pure, essential Zen alone, for even as a specific religious cult Zen employs forms and symbols, and the normal *structure* of the Buddhist religion. For pure life expresses itself within and through structure. Life without structure is unseen; it is the unmanifested Absolute. But structure without life is dead, and religion has altogether too much of this death.

For the ordinary religious consciousness grasps too much, and has too little faith in the actual present fact of the Life of life as the most all-absorbing and self-evident reality of our existence.

> Like unto space it knows no boundaries;
> Yet it is right here with us, ever retaining its
>   serenity and fullness;
> It is only when you seek it that you lose it.
> You cannot take hold of it, nor can you get rid
>   of it;
> While you can do neither, it goes on its own
>   way;
> You remain silent and it speaks; you speak and
>   it is silent;
> The great gate of charity is wide open with no
>   obstructions whatever before it.*

---

*   Hsuan-chiao, *Cheng-tao Ke*, 34. In Suzuki, *Manual of Zen*, p. 115.

BIBLIOGRAPHY

Anesaki, Masaharu. *History of Japanese Religion*. London, 1930.

Chu Ch'an. *The Huang Po Doctrine of Universal Mind*. London, 1947.

Eliot, Sir Charles. *Japanese Buddhism*. London, 1935.

First Zen Institute of America. *Cat's Yawn*. New York, 1947.

Gatenby, E. V. *The Cloud Men of Yamato*. London, 1929.

Grosse, Ernst. *Die Ostasiatische Tuschmalerei*. Berlin, 1923.

Hu Shih. "The Development of Zen Buddhism in China." Art. in *Chinese Political and Social Review*, vol. 15, no. 4. Peiping, January 1932.

Nukariya, Kaiten. *The Religion of the Samurai*. London, 1913.

Ohasama, S. and Faust, A. *Zen, der lebendige Buddhismus in Japan*. Gotha, 1925.

Okamura, K. *The Book of Tea*. Edinburgh, 1919. New York, 1926.

Senzaki, Nyogen and Reps, Paul. *The Gateless Gate* (A Translation of the *Mumon-kan*). Los Angeles, 1934.

———. *101 Zen Stories*. Philadelphia, n.d.

Shaku, Soyen. *Sermons of a Buddhist Abbot*. Chicago, 1906.

Steinilber-Oberlin, E. and Matsuo, Kuni. *Les Sectes boudhiques japonaises*. Paris, 1930.

Suzuki, B. L. *Mahayana Buddhism*. London, 1938.

Suzuki, D. T. *Essays in Zen Buddhism*, 3 vols. London and Kyoto, 1927, 1933, 1934.

———. *Die Grosse Befreiung* (German translation of the above, with an introduction by C. G. Jung). Leipzig, 1939.

———. *An Introduction to Zen Buddhism*. Kyoto, 1934.

———. *Manual of Zen Buddhism* (Selections from original texts). Kyoto, 1935.

———. *The Training of the Zen Buddhist Monk*. Kyoto, 1934.

———. *Zen Buddhism and Its Influence on Japanese Culture*. Kyoto, 1938.

Watts, Alan W. *The Collected Letters of Alan Watts*. Edited by Joan Watts and Anne Watts. Novato, CA: New World Library, 2017.

———. *The Spirit of Zen*. London, 1948.

Wong Mou-Lam. *The Sutra of Wei Lang (or Hui-neng)* (New edition, edited by Christmas Humphreys). London, 1944.

THE DRAWINGS AND SYMBOLS

Title page: The Chinese character for "Zen."

Page 19: Bodhidharma, after the painting by Soga Jasoku. Japanese, 15th century.

Page 25: The word AUM or OM, written in Sanskrit. This word is employed in both Hinduism and Mahayana Buddhism to denote the ultimate Reality.

Page 31: The Chinese character for "Tao."

Page 37: The Chinese yang-yin symbol, denoting the manifestation of the Tao in the pairs of opposites — light and dark, life and death, male and female, positive and negative.

Page 43: Bamboo, after the painting by Chu Lu (1553–1632). Chinese. Many references to the bamboo appear in Zen literature, and it is a favorite subject of Zen painters. A verse which describes the Zen life says: "The bamboo shadows are sweeping the stairs, but no dust is stirred."

Page 59: The Chinese characters for "wu hsin" (Japanese "mushin"), literally — "no mind." This is a special term for the Zen consciousness which it is impossible to render in any one English phrase. It might be said that the whole art of Zen is in learning to understand the difference between *wu hsin* and mere empty-mindedness or unconsciousness. *Wu hsin* is the psychological equivalent of Sunyata, the "solid" or creative void which effortlessly produces and embraces the universe.

Page 65: The Bamboo cutter, supposed to represent Huineng, the Sixth Patriarch. After the painting by Liang K'ai. Chinese, 13th century.

Page 71: From an autograph by the late Abbot Kozuki of Empukuji, Kyoto. Within the circle of the Void (Sunyata) is written: "Not one thing inside."

ABOUT THE AUTHOR

ALAN WATTS IS BEST KNOWN as an interpreter of Zen Buddhism in particular and of Indian and Chinese philosophy in general. He earned the reputation of being one of the most original and unfettered philosophers of the twentieth century. He was the author of more than twenty books, including *The Way of Zen*, *The Wisdom of Insecurity*, *Does It Matter?*, *Psychotherapy East and West*, *The Book*, *This Is It*, *The Joyous Cosmology*, *In My Own Way*, and *Tao: The Watercourse Way* (with Chungliang Al Huang). He died in 1973.